The Captain

A Parable of the Hidden Treasure

Story by Marty Chiu

Published by Wealth in Family

Marty@wealthinfamily.com

www.wealthinfamily.com

Printed and bound in the United States of America

ISBN: 978-0-578-70908-6

Dedication

To all family leaders who desire to keep their family unity and family wealth together for multiple generations.

This was the part of sailing that the Captain loved the most: he and his crew had come to this little island in the middle of the ocean for one thing: TREASURE, and they had found it. But something was different about this success. He didn't feel as successful as he usually did.

"Throw it in the hull with the rest of it,"
the Captain told his crew, as he sat
down on a log to rest his old knees.
He let the treasure map fall to his feet.

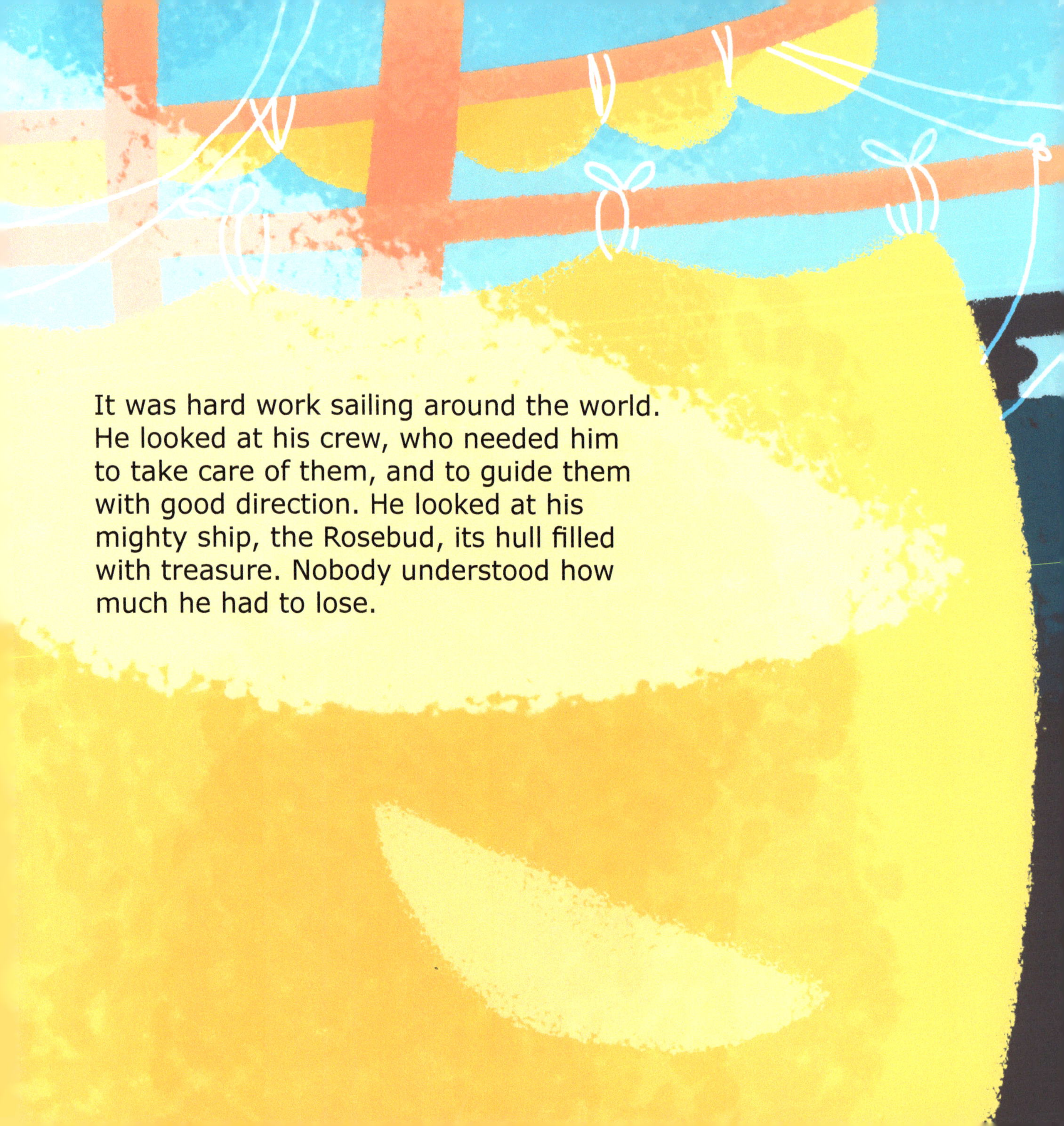

It was hard work sailing around the world. He looked at his crew, who needed him to take care of them, and to guide them with good direction. He looked at his mighty ship, the Rosebud, its hull filled with treasure. Nobody understood how much he had to lose.

The crew loaded up their ship,
and they were on their way,
in search of their next adventure.

That night, the Captain dreamed, as he often did, that his ship had silently struck a rock.

As they sailed on over the deep ocean, he lost his gold, coin by coin, and nobody noticed until it was too late, until the hull was almost empty and the ship was sinking...

The next morning,
the Captain woke up,
achy from sleeping
in the same old creaky bed.
He finally decided that
he was done sailing
the earth for treasure.
He called the crew together.

“I’ve decided that we
are finished hunting
for treasure.”
Everyone gasped.
“But Captain!”
said a young sailor,
“We can’t be stoppin’ now!”
“Yeah,” added a salty
old sailor.

"Everyone knows the Rosebud
be the fastest, richest,
and BEST ship to sail the 7 seas!
What would they say if we were
to just up and throw in the mop?"
"Is it even possible to just stop?"
worried the cook.

"Yes, I'm the captain, and we can stop any time we want," the Captain grumbled.

"But what else will a bunch of sailors like us do?" asked the cook, who liked his job cooking at sea.

The Captain thought about it. For so long, he had only thought of one thing: being the best. Having the best crew, sailing faster, farther, and getting the most treasure. And he had done very well at this. He had more treasure than he could ever spend.

"I don't know," replied the old Captain.
"Well," the First Mate said, after a pause, "What else do you like doin', Captain?"

The Captain hadn't thought about what he liked to do in a long time. Instantly, he thought back to his life before he was a captain. Nobody on the ship knew, but he had had a wife, and a little boy back home.

When his little boy was first born, something had changed inside of him. He had felt a deep need to give that boy everything. That's why he had taken off to sail the seas in search of treasure. He had wanted to be a big, strong man for his boy.

"Now look at yourself," the Captain thought. "Here you are in the middle of the ocean, with a ship full of treasure, and you've forgotten why you're out here in the first place! What good will a hull full of treasure do your son, if you never go back home to him?"

"We sail back home," the Captain said, surprised at how the word "home" felt on his lips.

"Home?!" the sailors turned to each other. Thinking about this made the big, tough men drop their hands to their sides and think about their mothers, wives, sons and daughters, for the first time in a long while. Once they had pulled themselves together, they turned their ship around and set a course back to England.

The crew sailed for many months, through many dangerous storms and wild adventures before the ship finally reached their homeland. When the Captain saw the coast of his home town, he was overcome with a mixed feeling of happiness, sadness, and fear of what he'd find, and what he'd have to say.

He disembarked and walked the path his feet slowly remembered, up the hill to his old house.

When he opened the door, he found his wife, much older than when he left. When she saw him, she dropped a bowl, and her look of shock slowly turned to a look of anger.

"How dare you come back! How can you ever make up for what you've put us through?"

The Captain did his best to explain, but he froze when his eyes settled on a little boy in a chair. "How can this be?" he stammered. "He looks just like he did the day I left!"

His wife was still angry. "Gone so long you can't recognize your own grandson!"

“My grandson!” The Captain’s eyes were moist as he slowly picked up the boy, who smiled with eyes that he thought looked like his own.

“Your son’s a man taller than you! He’ll be out mending the nets after the morning’s fishing. He’s finer at the rudder of a ship than even you, I reckon,” the wife said, picking up the bowl.

The Captain put down the boy, and gently left to find his son. Out by the water's edge, he saw the boy—the man, with tan, strong arms, and wide nets stretched out in the sun to dry.

As he walked up, the son recognized him slowly. "Father? Can it be?! But where did you come from? What great pains, what trials kept you from your own family all these years?"

"I..." And the Captain paused to catch his breath. "I set out to make a life for you, my boy. I sailed the oceans and fought harder than anyone else to fill my hull with treasure. I've come home at last to give you what I have gained."

The son shook his head in sadness and anger. "What filled my nights with tears and sighs was not a lack of treasure. You could have sailed back empty-handed! I hungered endlessly for the dad I never had! I would have given up all the treasure in the world if it meant that you were there for me just one of the times I needed you!"

"That's why I sailed back now, my boy." The Captain spoke slowly, sadly. "I am deeply sorry for the pain I caused you. I realized the real treasure of my family was hidden as I toiled for all of you. I saw that nothing mattered more than rebuilding bridges I may have burnt."

The Captain's words didn't seem to help. The two men went back to the son's home, where his wife was waiting, with a hot meal in the pot, young boy playing on the floor. She busied herself with her child and bedtime things, letting the Captain and her husband talk.

At first, nothing the Captain said could make his son less angry. He didn't give up, though. There was much to be said before the father and son could truly understand each other. The Captain listened to his son, who explained his successes, how he met his wife, how he grew to be the most respected fisherman in town (some said the best in England). The Captain, for his turn, told of how he built a crew, how he won huge treasures, lost even bigger ones, and came to long for the one treasure he left behind: his family. They spoke long into the night, and the sun began to rise before the two could finally look each other in the eye.

"Well, I'm glad you decided to come back," the boy finally admitted with emotion in his voice. "I am relieved to hear that," the Captain replied. "But what of all your treasure?"...

"Oh," the Captain said, having forgotten about his ship and crew. "It's all down in my ship, by the seaside."

And so, the whole family, father, son, and his wife, and the Captain's wife with grandson in arm, walked down toward the docks. The son hoped that they wouldn't find that the crew had sailed away in the night, with the treasure of a life's work. The Captain walked slowly and didn't seem to worry.

What they did see when they got there made them all smile. The crew were there, feet dangling over the side of the ship. The tough seamen had stayed up all night, each taking tearful turns, explaining their hometowns, and who they missed, and who they hoped to see.

The Captain asked the crew what they all wanted, and the First Mate spoke for all, "Captain, if it be your will, the men and I, red-eyed from rememberin' our mothers, sweethearts and babies we've long left, would like the chance to seek 'em out, in our own homes, as you have done. We don't be askin' no piece of yer treasure, just your leave to go."

The Captain clapped each man on the back, and still paid them a fair share from the vast hull's treasures. And when all had gone their way, there was still far more than a lifetime's worth left over.

"It's time, then," said the son, "to decide what to do next. We've got the fastest ship in the 7 seas."

"We've got the best fisherman in England," said the Captain.

"And more than a lifetime's worth of treasure, to spend or save as we see fit," added the son.

"We've also got a Captain who's getting a little too old for adventures," observed the Captain's wife, arms crossed, with admonition in her voice, and the Captain rubbed his tired eyes in agreement.

"I'm sure we can figure out a plan," said the son's wife. The family smiled, clasped hands, and walked homeward, where they all talked, planned together, laughed, cried, and the Captain ate the first hot breakfast he'd eaten in a long time.

A Message from the Author

The Captain returned at last to the hidden treasure that was most important to him: his family. The years he had spent at sea were lost opportunities for being present with his family and they had kept him from collecting memorable moments along the way. His ambitious pursuits ended up as a distraction, causing him to lose focus on what mattered most.

You may not be as absent as the Captain was, but you may find yourself disappointed, discouraged, and fatigued by the obstacles that keep your family from staying connected. You may want to create a positive impact in your family but don't know where to begin. Before you know it, years pass, and you worry that it is too late to create and sustain unity within your family.

Everyone will leave a legacy. What do you want yours to be?

- Maybe it is your intent to offer your family a better life with the assets you leave behind.
- Maybe you want your family to be happy and connected, communicating with honor and respect.
- Or maybe you want future generations to remember who you were and what values you stood for.

Your influence as a Family Leader is the cornerstone of your legacy.

If you are like Family Leaders I have worked with over the last few decades, making time to mentor and counsel the rising generation is not at the top of your priority list. Most families are led, but few are led on purpose.

If you desire a cohesive family unit, family members that communicate with honor and respect, and support each other both now and in the future, you'll need to be mindful, thoughtful, and intentional with your effort. You must decrease that which matters least in order to increase that which matters most.

At Wealth in Family, we prepare Family Leaders to build bridges of unity, sustain family continuity, and perpetuate a family's unique culture across multiple generations. We aim to shift the Family Leader's perspective in a way that makes a tremendous impact on future generations.

Personalized Services Available

We Work with You

In our six-week online course, we guide you through the important components of preparing and equipping the rising generation to receive their financial and emotional inheritance. We educate you on developing your leadership skills, emotional intelligence, communication skills, and create your custom-tailored Family Wealth Blueprint™.

Discover more about our online course and sign up for an introductory webinar at www.wealthinfamily.com.

We Work for You

A tailored service for Family Leaders looking for customized one-on-one engagement that will support you and your family. We coach and counsel you through the entire process, which includes facilitated conversations with you and your family, helping you navigate through challenges that arise.

If you are looking for one-on-one support, email us about an initial consultation at Marty@wealthinfamily.com.

"Coming together is a beginning, staying together is progress, and working together is success." —Henry Ford

About the Author

Marty Chiu's journey in life has been unusual. His childhood desire to be an entrepreneur caused him to challenge what was the typical career path. Although when choosing a major at California State University, Long Beach, he took the safe route and majored in mechanical engineering.

As he was about to begin his second year of college, he had a near-death experience that changed the direction of his life forever. While playing in the finals of a tennis tournament, he suffered a massive stroke that caused paralysis on the left side of his body. During his three-month hospital stay, there were complications, during which Marty's life hung in the balance. Throughout those difficult months, Marty contemplated his calling and decided to pursue it if he got the opportunity.

At the end of his hospital stay, the doctors said he would not be able to walk or play tennis again and would probably be confined to a wheelchair. Marty did his best to prove these predictions wrong. By God's grace and through Marty's perseverance, he was able to walk again and return to playing tennis. He took the first step toward his calling, changing his major, and graduated with a degree in finance and an intent to positively impact others.

Since 1988, Marty has stepped into his calling and is making a difference in people's lives by helping them appreciate what is most important to them and live more intentionally with the resources they possess. He is the founder of a unique holistic wealth management company, VantaQuest, that aligns a client's life, family, and finances with a purpose to create harmony in their life. He is also the founder of Wealth in Family, where he prepares Family Leaders to sustain family unity and wealth for multiple generations.

www.ingramcontent.com/pod-product-compliance
Lightning Source LLC
LaVergne TN
LVHW071238210926
848486LV00007B/293
9780578709086